WELCOME & THANK YOU!

Thank you for investing in *Compelling Selling: Simple & Profitable Techniques for Effective, Efficient Sales Conversations.*

I appreciate you, and because you're taking time to learn about the way people buy and the words you can use to connect with them quickly and authentically, I have a special gift for you. It's the AlikeAbility™ ScoreCard.

The ScoreCard gives you information about your Buying Style, your preferred way of messaging and receiving communication. Since we tend to sell the way we buy, it also provides a sneak preview into how you might normally approach prospects.

Knowing your dominant style will enable you to enjoy reading this book with a keen eye for:

- Learning how you behave.

- Learning how others perceive you.

- Figuring out where you differ from other styles.

- Determining your combination of the 4 Buying Styles.

- Other surprises about yourself, how you buy and sell.

It takes less than 5 minutes to complete! And the information lasts a lifetime! Visit:

CompellingSellingBook.com/resources

PRAISE FOR
COMPELLING SELLING!

"Research shows that understanding of your own style as well as others is very important to building better relationships in personal and professional life. Mismatched communication styles can lead to conflict, and in selling, it can lead to lost sales. Using a communication style other people find difficult to understand can mean the difference between failure and success in sales. Good communication opens doors..., and poor communication closes them. And while there are many factors involved in sales success, the data shows that communication is the single most important key to success.

"Nancy Zare's new book, *Compelling Selling: Simple & Profitable Techniques for Effective, Efficient Sales Conversations*, is a brilliantly concise guide to finding the exact language that converts prospects into customers. And the way she does that is by leveraging communication profiles.

"The greatest value from communication styles, in my opinion, is understanding them well enough that you notice them in others and using them to communicate in a way that makes it easier for your message to get received.

"And in that vein, Nancy Zare has done something amazing—condensed that process into a 100-page book that helps you identify, understand and leverage 4 manageable communication styles. I am trained in Meyer-Briggs® (which I love), but 16 profiles is way too much for practical application in selling. Nancy Zare's scientific work has made leveraging communication profiles for sales both manageable and easily applied.

"In fact, the book is packed with insightful ideas and examples that are immediately applicable in virtually all sales environments. This is Occam's razor for communication styles, and all communicators will benefit from reading it.

"*Compelling Selling: Simple & Profitable Techniques for Effective, Efficient Sales Conversations* is a short, easy read that is big on value and that I would recommend to anyone who communicates for a living. 5 stars."

James Muir
An Amazon Verified Purchase

ALSO BY DR. NANCY ZARE

Words That Sell with Style

Closing More Sales:
Introduction to AlikeAbility™ System

Workplace Hostility: Myth and Reality
With Co-Author Gerald W. Lewis

COMPELLING SELLING

Simple & Profitable Techniques for Effective,
Efficient Sales Conversations

DR. NANCY ZARE

DISCLAIMER:

While all attempts have been made to verify information provided in this publication, neither the author nor the publisher assumes any responsibility for errors, omissions or contradictory interpretation of the subject matter herein. This publication is designed to provide accurate and authoritative information with regards to the subject matter covered. However, it is sold with the understanding that the author and the publisher are not engaged in rendering legal, accounting, or other professional advice. If professional advice or other expert assistance is required, the services of a competent professional should be sought. The purchaser or reader of this publication assumes responsibility for the use of these materials and information. Adherence to all applicable laws and regulations, including federal, state and local, governing professional licensing, business practices, advertising and any other aspects of doing business is the sole responsibility of the purchaser or reader.

CONTENTS

This book is dedicated to my Mom, Dorothy Amdur Zare
(DAZzling Diamond) who loved Words.

CHAPTER 1

WELCOME!

June runs a successful social media business. She met a prospect online and they hit it off immediately. After a series of text messages, the prospect expressed an interest in June's services.

So she prepared and sent a proposal outlining how she would enhance the prospect's presence on four of the key platforms plus her payment schedule. A day passed with no response. Then another.

June texted the prospect inquiring if the proposal had been received. Again silence. She was positive that they had shared a common outlook and the prospect wanted help. What changed? What to do? How could she proceed with getting hired and starting the job?

Has this ever happened to you? You meet someone, start a relationship, receive positive recognition, identify an issue, present a solution, and then the prospect disappears. If you're speaking in-person, you might hear an objection, such as, "I'll have to think about it," followed by an end to the conversation.

However, when the communication has been digital, the most common response is ghosting—the prospect simply vanishes and gives no reply.

When a vibrant relationship goes quiet, there is usually something that went wrong. Can you spot June's mistake? It's one of the most common one that trips up coaches, consultants, and solopreneurs. What do you think it is? Could it be any of the following reasons?

- June didn't identify the prospect's needs sufficiently.

- She misestimated the prospect's interest.

- She failed to establish a viable working relationship.

- She should have asked more questions.

- She needed to communicate better her value to the prospect.

June is my client, and she consulted me right away about what to do. As a sales psychologist, I use my knowledge of human behavior to identify how people make buying decisions and advise what approach to take and the words to use that lead to getting hired.

The first step we took together was to look up the prospect on social media and diagnose her buying style. The individual's broad, warm smile, casual clothing, and chatty text messages are characteristic of the #4 buying style, i.e., people who seek harmony and are friendly, trusting, and easy-going. This is an individual who values relationships first and foremost and who buys connections.

June is a people person, and that quality enabled her and the prospect to bond initially. However, when asking for the sale, she became very sales-oriented. All her energy was directed towards getting hired so she could begin the project. Her proposal lacked the warm, fuzzy qualities that characterized their initial exchanges.

While many factors could have been behind *the prospect's silence, the major mistake that hijacked* the sale was a mismatch in communication styles.

Bottom line, she stepped out of rapport with the prospect.

With this in mind, I advised June to text the prospect with the message that no matter what decision was made, she wanted to maintain a friendship. Within five minutes, the prospect returned a text message, and the relationship was back on track.

Shortly thereafter, June did get hired and is working with this customer.

Should June use the same approach with every potential client? No. She must adjust what she says to suit the other person's buying style. Most of her clientele respond best to her message of efficiency and results. Others appreciate when she offers caring and support. She also has clients who appreciate her wealth of information and her systematic and professional way of delivering services.

With my guidance, June now chooses her words to match the prospect, and her practice is thriving. Her calendar is filled.

Knowing the prospect's buying style and shifting your communication accordingly is the premise behind *Compelling Selling: Simple & Profitable Tips for Effective, Efficient Sales Conversations*. Identify the other person's values, match it, and you'll get hired.

Who Should Read This Book?

Compelling Selling: Simple & Profitable Tips for Effective, Efficient Sales Conversations is a reference manual for coaches, consultants, and trusted advisors in the service professions who are responsible for acquiring their own book of business. If you are a small business owner or entrepreneur who is seeking to be hired, you'll benefit from this book's approach.

In addition, marketing personnel responsible for creating websites, developing social media posts, designing logos and illustrations, and writing copy will appreciate applying the principles from this book. If you're seeking to fill sales funnels and convert leads into clients, then you're in the business of sales and need to know how to build rapport quickly and authentically with all buying styles!

What Is Sales?

Do you view yourself as a salesperson? Most service professionals don't as they identify solely with their occupations. However, if you provide a service and influence people to take some kind of action (especially choosing to become and remain a customer), these behaviors qualify you as a salesperson.

Most of my clients find the act of selling daunting. They much prefer to do their "work" and shy away from sales. They may have chosen their profession, in part, because they thought of sales as manipulative and counter to their desire to serve people.

Ironically, sales is service! Helping prospects figure out their problems and offer solutions is exactly the heart of selling. Regardless of whether the individual accepts your specific approach, you have provided a worthwhile service by defining the problem and exploring options.

So, what is sales? Sales is defined as an exchange of energy. Your energy takes the form of the services you provide. Your prospect's energy takes the form of money. To consummate the sale, you influence the prospect to take the action of hiring you.

How do we influence others? There are many methods. The tool used most reliably in today's society is language, the words chosen when speaking and writing. These words (and phrases) are the means most readily available to persuade people to take action. Select the right words and people respond in the way you want. Utter the wrong words and you may turn off the individual as illustrated by June's experience.

A Common Mistake

Before we met, June communicated from a one-size-fits-all sales approach. *This is the most common mistake most people make in seeking to get hired.* We **assume** that others think, decide, speak, and act the way we do. We project onto them our thoughts and feelings. Then we are surprised, disappointed, even upset when they don't behave as we anticipated.

Because we wrongfully think that others are operating from the same communication style, when the prospect hesitates, we think the reasonable response is to repeat the substance of our message. We say the original idea more loudly or write with more emphasis. Rather than "break through," this same approach and style turns off the other person, and then we wonder what went wrong. The roadblock is that we are stuck in one way of communicating.

The reality is that people operate from different personality styles. These styles determine to a large extent how they communicate. Through the years, research has shown that there are four distinct ways of behaving. And while everyone is a combination of all four, usually one is dominant in a business context, and a different one is dominant in social situations.

Those individuals who have the ability to read the other person's style and adjust accordingly, as June did the second time around, have a full caseload and a robust practice. This skill, I call **AlikeAbility**, can be acquired through study and practice. Regardless of the prospect's style, by selecting the right words to convey your message, you can build rapport quickly and authentically so that the other person is more likely to hire you.

To develop this skill takes knowledge and practice. According to Malcolm Gladwell, 10,000 hours or more are required to become a "natural." If you're eager to speed up this process and shorten your learning curve the book you are now reading, *Compelling Selling: Simple & Profitable Tips for Effective, Efficient Sales Conversations* can help.

It provides the words and phrases that enhance the probability of creating connections quickly and authentically with each personality style. For those who prefer a video format, you'll also find my course, *Selling with Styles*, to be extremely helpful in mastering this material.

Overview

In the pages that follow, you find information on each of the 4 buying styles listed with a quick phrase that describes their buying mode. Their main values are listed along with synonyms. Use any of these words in your written or oral communication, and you can be assured that your prospect will respond in a positive manner that builds rapport authentically and moves the relationship towards doing business together.

Even the best words may not result in the buyer's decision to buy. With the pandemic of 2020, buying patterns are steadily shifting from in-person transactions to online. The number of touchpoints needed for buyers to say "yes" is growing. This is especially true for intangible services. So that you don't leave money on the table, it's essential that you follow up. With this in mind, I've also included some bonus material focused on how to follow up with each of the four styles of buyers.

Finally, I've provided some material about selling styles. If you are seeking to sell more effectively and get hired readily, it's imperative to shift your style to match that of the buyer as well as downplay or discard the common mistakes made by each of the selling styles.

Invitation

If you like the idea of adjusting your style to suit the prospect, join other like-minded people in Relationship Builderz for Sales Success, a Facebook group for entrepreneurs, business owners, and marketing professionals.

Based on the Platinum Rule, Relationship Builderz for Sales Success provides a forum for learning about buying styles, selling styles, and developing approaches that connect quickly and authentically to convert prospects into clients. You'll also receive tips on how to apply the information in this book.

Before we dive into the 4 Buying Styles, find out what is your dominant buying style. I recommend you take the AlikeAbility ScoreCard at:

CompellingSellingBook.com/resources

.

CHAPTER 2

ALIKEABILITY SYSTEM AND THE 4 BUYING STYLES

The AlikeAbility System is a 5-step process for reading the buyer's personality style and adjusting your own to match it. It consists of these steps:

1. Define 4 buying styles.
2. Determine your dominant sales style.
3. Diagnose the prospect's buying style.
4. Duplicate or match the prospect's buying style.
5. Downplay and discard the part of your sales style that's a disconnect.

The AlikeAbility System is based on the **Platinum Rule**. Most people are familiar with the Golden Rule: Treat others the way you want to be treated. The Platinum Rule, which I first learned from Tony Alessandra, states: Treat others the way they want to be treated. The most common mistake most people make is that of assuming that other individuals think, decide and behave alike. Instead, it's vital to communicate with others on their terms.

While it is logical that we'll catch more flies with honey than vinegar, many people protest that they don't want to change themselves to fit someone else. Why? Because they believe this shift would be a violation of their integrity. Not so. Treating others the way they prefer is humanity at its finest.

Bear in mind, everyone is a combination of all 4 styles, just in different proportions and amounts. Consequently, we each have the capacity to bring to the forefront that part of ourselves which genuinely matches our prospect. Communicating with language that enables the other person to grasp the meaning of our message more easily just makes common sense.

Moreover, the way to raise AlikeAbility is by emphasizing values. Each style values things differently. Yet all values are valuable. Thus, you never have to compromise who you are to connect quickly and authentically with other people.

Four Personality Styles

The theory that there are four personality styles was first proposed by Hippocrates, the father of modern medicine. He observed that his patients presented with four distinct bodily and psychological states. He called them temperaments.

This early science has given way to many personality systems. Some of the better-known ones are DiSC®, Myers-Briggs®, and the Wilcox Learning System. You may also have been introduced to colors, birds, dogs, sea creatures, and objects. At last count, there are over 200 such personality systems. What is notable is that their common characteristic is having four distinct styles.

The system used in *Compelling Selling: Simple & Profitable Tips for Effective, Efficient Sales Conversations* is called **SHOE**. It's a combination of numbers, colors and words that differentiate the four styles. The order reflects the number of contacts needed to make a buying decision, from 1–2 touch points for the fast, decisive style, to well over 8 interactions for the studious, thoughtful buyer. For brevity's sake, the styles can be identified as: **#2, #4, #6** and **#8**.

Contacts can be tangible, such as person-to-person meetings, cards and gifts. Or they can be digital, such as email, voice and text messages. Indirect touch points count as a half-contact, which is why it often takes much more outreach to close a sale.

SHOE is an acronym I chose as a shorthand and cute way of remembering the styles. When speaking to audiences and working with clients, I help them *"walk" in the SHOES of their prospects.*

The acronym is made from these words. Buyers are compelled to be:

S=Successful, H=Harmonious, O=Orderly, and **E=Educated**. Each style is distinguished by a collection of values, likes, and dislikes that are shared by the large majority of people who make up this type.

Note that no one is a "pure" style. We are all a combination of each of the four styles, just in different amounts and a different order. Moreover, most people rely on one style when making decisions in their work life and another style when being social. Our style changes according to context.

Because people tend to sell the way they buy, I have emphasized buying styles. However, each of the styles can also be detected by how someone sells. In parentheses, I have also listed a quick reference word for this person's selling style.

#2 Successful Buyers
(Transactional Sellers)

The #2 Successful Buyers are driven to experience life to its fullest. Within one to two contacts, they are ready to make a purchase. Novelty, adventure, and opportunity spur them to act quickly and decisively. They make spontaneous and impulsive decisions.

They disdain limits of any sort, seeking to exercise their freedom to do, be, and have anything they desire.

Highly competitive, #2 Successful Buyers are driven to succeed and yet have fun doing it. Life is a game and they keep score by accumulating tangible tokens of their victories as well as that of status and public recognition. To come out on top, they readily flex themselves and make adjustments and changes.

Because they make snap buying decisions, they respond well to one-time offers, urgency, time deadlines, and scarcity. #2 Successful Buyers fear missing out. Sellers love them for their quick selection time, but be warned, they are just as likely to choose something unrelated once the impulse to buy has been ignited.

Examples of #2 Successful Buyers

Desiree—dressed all in black, you might think that Desiree's personality was quiet. Far from it! The dark, skin-tight jumpsuit only served as a neutral background to display her love of jewels and attract attention.

Her blonde hair was gathered in a fashionable bun, fastened by a diamond-studded comb. As she gracefully moved through the room, her gold, dangle earrings that reflected the light mesmerized the viewer. Her eyes were heavily etched in black, and her lips, full and beckoning, were outlined in bright crimson.

Desiree wore open-toed, patent-leather stiletto heels. What stood out most, however, was her fire-engine red handbag with the large, gold clasp. Its shape was a cross between a crocodile and lion decorated with Swarovski® crystals. It was her signature piece, which she proudly described in a loud, fast paced voice to a circle of admiring acquaintances.

Her business card was almost as striking as her appearance. On a gold matte, extra-thick card stock were etched black letters proclaiming her company name and title. On the opposite side, it read:

"Yes! You are unique and special, and we are a reflection of you!"

Desiree cares intensely about her image and enjoys drawing attention to herself. She wants only the best things in life as she moves quickly from activity to activity. She is impulsive, spontaneous and often scattered because she is constantly multitasking. However, she's fun to be with, decidedly sexy, and definitely the life of the party.

Kevin—enjoys standing out in a crowd. He likes wearing colors, fabrics and accessories that grab attention and make a statement. He relishes driving a car with its customized license plate that advertises his business. He freely tells you that it's a fool who keeps to himself and remains invisible.

In school, Kevin struggled with reading, memorization and conduct. He's a hands-on type of guy who learns best by doing. Action is his middle name as he rarely sits still. He's constantly on the go and has a tightly packed schedule. As a result, he often arrives in the parking lot at the appointed hour and is late when he actually makes his appearance at the meeting. His hearty hello, broad smile and quick, vigorous handshake usually silence any criticism. However, he's quick to express displeasure, blow up on a dime, and just as readily resume his easy-going nature.

Kevin is very charismatic and an exceptional storyteller. He loves that people flock to him. He's entertaining and lively as he recounts events in his life. As you listen, you suspect that his narrative brings out the sensational and dramatic. With a poker face, he assures everyone that, "This is exactly how it happened."

Not surprisingly, Kevin is into sales. Although details and paperwork are not his thing, he appreciates talking with prospects and gets a thrill from negotiating. He chases the victory of closing a deal, and it doesn't matter to him what merchandise or service he represents. He always wants to do so with pizzazz and finesse. He's driven to succeed.

Find out your dominant Buying Style. Take the AlikeAbility ScoreCard at

CompellingSellingBook.com/resources

#4 Harmonious Buyers
(Relational Sellers)

Being in a relationship, forming a bond, connecting authentically, sharing fully, doing something of significance, and contributing to a greater purpose are the motivating factors for #4 Harmonious Buyers. They care passionately about people and causes. They freely volunteer and often play a supporting role, especially where they can be involved in the community and charitable work.

#4 Harmonious Buyers avoid tension, conflict, and arguments. Instead, they desire peace, harmony, and collaboration. They make up their minds relatively quickly with 3–4 contacts. However, if they feel they have been treated as a transaction, they get cold feet, cancel appointments, fail to show, return or void the purchase, and widely broadcast their displeasure.

Add +1 to the number of touch points required for #4 Harmonious Buyers. Within 24 hours of saying "yes," you must reconnect and assure them that being friends is what you most care about. They must feel a connection with the seller before they can make a buying decision because their biggest fear is being an object, a transaction.

Examples of #4 Harmonious Buyers

Carolyn—has always cared about people. Throughout her life, her first thoughts were how to serve and be helpful. In school, she studied psychology and later became a psychotherapist. Additional coursework led her to earn several certifications in specialized treatment modalities.

Following her graduate degree, Carolyn accepted work in a clinic. However, the long hours and low pay motivated her to open a private practice. She quickly discovered that running a business was quite different than treating clients. Her biggest challenge has been to market her services and ask to get hired. Not being spurred by materialism, she developed a sliding fee scale. Occasionally, she does not charge for a session and is very generous with her time.

Carolyn dresses in loose, flowy garments, such as a multicolored paisley skirt (her favorite), pastel blouse and Birkenstock sandals. Her makeup is minimal, just foundation and blush. She wears her hair long and straight. Numerous bangle bracelets plus dangle earrings complete the ensemble.

She greets everyone with a warm smile, twinkling eyes, and extended hands which quickly pull the other person into an embrace. Carolyn laughs easily and has a light, playful spirit. She passes out compliments readily as she often expresses gratitude and appreciation for everyone and everything. Her sing-song voice registers full volume and is moderately fast.

Carolyn is an excellent conversationalist, encouraging others to share by providing rapt attention. A diplomat, she chooses her words carefully, making sure that her comments encourage and uplift. Later, she reflects deeply about her exchanges and demeanor, wondering if she could have done things better. She loves to read and discuss books on personal growth.

Despite her lack of funds, she gives to several charities, especially of her time. She supports environmental causes and recycles everything.

Eduardo—made a choice early in life, which has served him well as an adult. While still in high school, he was told by his guidance counselor that his profile and academic performance and interests fit several career paths, including doctor, lawyer, and accountant. At the age of 17, he reflected that he could become a good doctor or lawyer; however, he knew that being a husband and father mattered most to him. So he decided to pursue a degree in business as he thought it would afford him more quality time with loved ones.

Now a CPA, what Eduardo enjoys most about his work are the hours he spends interacting with clients.

He has cultivated a habit of checking with them at least three times a year, not just at tax season. By visiting them at work, he gains a better understanding of their business and personal challenges. This enables him to give expert advice about their financial activities. In addition, this low-key strategy also cements relationships so that his client retention rate is 98%.

To maintain his credentials, Eduardo spends more than 100 hours a year in pursuit of continuing education. He thoroughly enjoys attending professional conferences where he can meet colleagues and catch up with old friends. When he returns to work, nothing pleases him more than to mentor some of the younger associates in the firm. Recently he was asked to give a series of lectures within the agency. A bit shy, Eduardo was grateful that only a few people attended because he hates taking center stage and would have felt tongue-tied talking to a large group. When he speaks, he sounds like a warm bubble bath as there's something comforting and soothing about his voice.

Eduardo is a person of integrity. Although it is expected of him to bring in new business to his firm, he is candid in telling prospects the truth, even if that means losing them as clients. If their tax returns were prepared properly and with less cost than he could have done, he tells them honestly to stay with their current CPA. He wants what is best for them, without thoughts of himself.

In keeping with his casual outlook, Eduardo avoids dressing in suits or suit jackets. Instead, he wears khakis, pastel shirt, no tie, and a sweater vest. His shoes have a well-worn look, and his dark glasses frame his face, which is clean-shaved. He keeps his dark hair on the longer side and is grateful that it remains thick and wavy.

Weekends are spent with family. He loves having a date night with his spouse and Sunday dinners with the extended clan. During the spring and summer, he coaches Little League. Life is good, and he makes time to worship on a regular basis.

Find out your dominant Buying Style. Take the AlikeAbility ScoreCard at

CompellingSellingBook.com/resources

#6 Orderly Buyers
(Procedural Sellers)

Keeping things the same is the fervent desire of #6 Orderly Buyers. They value stability, solidarity, structure, systems, process, rules, directions, instructions, guidelines, and governance. In a word, they like control, internal and external. They dislike change and work fervently to keep things the same.

#6 Orderly Buyers appreciate the status quo and defer to how things have always been. They like conservative, classic, traditional products and services. They tend to buy local within their own community and country. New and improved invoke suspicion and guardedness.

It takes 5 or more touch points for the #6 Orderly Buyers to review your company's reputation and observe your professionalism. The way to guide them to make a buying decision is by sharing testimonials, historical documentation, positive public reports, and a solid record from the Better Business Bureau. Their greatest fear is receiving something unexpected because they failed to read the fine print. They intensely dislike surprises.

Examples of #6 Orderly Buyers

Barbara—it was 4:01 PM and Barbara telephoned the business acquaintance to see if she had made a mistake in the time or place where they were to meet. She had been sitting at the coffee shop easily 10 minutes or more prior to the appointed time of 4:00 PM. She wore a dark, navy blue suit, pale yellow blouse, a single strand of pearls and stud earrings. She carried a small purse plus an organizer and a briefcase. Her pumps were polished and matched the purse in color.

The gentleman arrived just as Barbara rang. This provoked a laugh from both of them as they exchanged a formal handshake and sat down. After a few minutes of pleasantries—weather and traffic conditions—they got right to business.

Barbara had a list of things she wished to discuss and asked a question at the start of the conversation. She listened respectfully, and where appropriate, she repeated an idea or added her perspective. She took notes. There were no lags in the conversation, and she never interrupted the other speaker. Her voice was moderate in volume and speed and had a pleasant tone and pitch.

Barbara expressed an interest in the services outlined by the other party. She inquired about the cost and delivery. Most importantly, she asked for the terms and conditions to be specified in a written document. The business acquaintance assured her she would receive it the next day.

Everything in order, Barbara gathered her items into her briefcase and stood up. She offered her hand before leaving. She picked up the used coffee cup and napkin, depositing them in the waste bin on the way out. The place was as immaculate, perhaps even cleaner, than when she first arrived.

Barbara got into her budget-friendly, 10-year old car, which looked almost as new as the day she bought it. Everything was in its place, and she proceeded to drive to the exit from the parking lot. She made a complete stop, looked both ways, looked again, and cautiously drove into the street. On the way home, she obeyed all traffic rules and regulations.

A reserved person, Barbara greeted her teenaged children with a nod and smile. Then she prepared dinner for the family, cleaned up, collected the trash (it's Tuesday and pick-up happens early Wednesday mornings), then watched television with her spouse until bedtime. This routine continues; each day is carefully planned and executed. Barbara doesn't like to be surprised and prefers things to remain orderly and safe.

John—was one of the first people to arrive at the networking event, and he announced with satisfaction that he has been with the same company for 32 years. With job changes the norm, it's rare to meet someone with such longevity. Loyalty means a great deal to him, and he's proud to have given service to this banking institution. He anticipates remaining there until he retires in another 5 years.

As expected of a bank representative, John wore a charcoal gray suit, ivory shirt, conservative tie, and a matching hankie. A service pin glistened from his lapel. Despite it being after business hours, he looks as if he walked freshly from the dry cleaners.

He's comfortable conversing with most people, observing all social amenities, and putting others at ease by asking for their occupation. John greeted people with an outstretched hand, gave a firm handshake, looked directly in the other person's eyes, and stated his name. It was a well-practiced habit followed by asking for the other individual's information and then talking about the venue or the host.

John's business cards are nestled neatly in a metal case bearing his initials. Next to his name are his credentials. If you were to visit his office, you would find his degrees neatly framed and hung on the wall. His desktop is nearly bare as most paperwork is filed in cabinets or organized on the computer. Only what he needs at the moment resides on his desk.

John values stability both at work and home. He is happily married to his wife of 30 years. They have two adult children, both married, and he's excited to announce the birth of their first grandchild. They have already planned a trip to visit the newborn, who he gifted with a college fund.

Not one to take risks, John lives within a 20-mile radius of where he was born. He even went to college and graduate school in-state. When making purchases, he exercises frugality, and more often than not, buys brand-name items, always within budget, mostly paying cash. Although he doesn't say so, he's disappointed in his adult daughter who seems to be a spender, because he's definitely a saver.

Find out your dominant Buying Style. Take the AlikeAbility ScoreCard at

CompellingSellingBook.com/resources

#8 Educated Buyers
(Informational Sellers)

#8 Educated Buyers value learning, information, research, logic, analysis, and rationality. They appreciate intelligence, competence, mastery, expertise, and are big picture thinkers. They like to read, reflect, solve problems, invent, and take a deep nosedive into a subject matter.

When #8 Educated Buyers make a decision to purchase something, it's vital that they be thoroughly informed and educated. Being "smart" as a buyer is essential as they fear making a wrong decision based on having too little evidence or being outright duped.

#8 Educated Buyers feel compelled to read and understand everything they can about the proposed purchase, which is why they delay in going forward and saying yes. Pressure them in any way and they immediately walk away from the deal, even though they truly needed and wanted it. Analysis paralysis often overtakes them as they keep gathering information as long as possible. A good strategy is to have them agree to a deadline, and then let them think about it without interruption.

Examples of #8 Educated Buyers

Edith—from her occupation as a personal trainer, you might guess that Edith cares about people. Upon further investigation, it isn't so. She left the field of IT because it was negatively impacting her health. To address aging, she began working out, found she enjoyed it, and later became certified to teach. Exercising gets her in the zone. Working with people is something she accepts as part of her job, freely admitting that she's uncomfortable in large groups.

Edith is super intelligent and can tell you everything you wanted to know about body mechanics. Nothing pleases her more than to inform clients why a particular exercise achieves flexibility or muscle mass and the reason behind sequencing certain activities. She excels in this type of instruction.

Because of her keen observational powers, Edith has learned that while working out, some clients prefer explanation, whereas others like to be distracted. One individual craves stimulation and variety, but another likes to follow a routine. She is smart enough to shift the exercise activities once she understands these preferences, which explains why she has a successful, private practice. If it weren't for her current clients telling friends, she would be struggling to fill her calendar because she intensely dislikes selling.

Although she was attending a professional networking event, Edith arrived in her gym clothes and sneakers. That made sense to her because afterwards she would be working with clients. Even when not on the job, she has her go-to outfit, a kind of uniform that saves time having to think about what to wear. She had no makeup, jewelry or watch, and her hair was simply pulled back with a clip. Despite most people milling around and meeting one another, she seated herself solo at a table and made little eye contact with those standing nearby. When approached by one of the attendees, she didn't offer a smile or handshake, although she did accept it from the other person, giving a soft hand in turn.

Once engaged in conversation, Edith asked lots of questions about the topic. She was inquisitive and soaked up ideas. She perked up when learning something new. Yet she was content with long silences and didn't have any need to fill empty spaces by asking about the other person. Her voice was slow and soft, with lots of pauses as she sought the exact word to say.

When she was ready, Edith departed without a backward glance. There was no ceremony, no cordial words about "nice to meet you" or "let's stay in touch." She was relieved to find her car and drive directly to the gym. The stop sign slowed her acceleration only slightly as she noted that there was no other traffic to heed, and thus drove straight through the intersection.

Edith lives a quiet life with her husband and 3 cats. She enjoys gardening, reading, and scrabble. They have season tickets to the symphony.

Larry—undeniably, Larry is an expert in his field of cosmetology. He earned this designation from over 30 years in the business and the numerous contributions he has made to the industry through his innovative products and techniques. He has been recognized both locally and nationally. Celebrities flock to his salon for his service. The walls of his shop display photos of them along with praise for his work. An album sits in the waiting area with numerous, yellowed newspaper clippings extolling his achievements.

Working in a salon, Larry dresses the same each day, khaki trousers, white shirt, and a white lab coat. He wears sturdy, leather shoes that are well-worn, horn-rimmed glasses, and a plain wristwatch. He drives a hybrid vehicle because it gets good gas mileage.

Being smarter than most people, Larry has little tolerance for those who fail to learn quickly. He despises incompetence. He is a quick study. Once he has figured out how to do something, he expects others to master the task in a short time and doesn't allow for any mistakes.

Larry loves to debate and is constantly educating himself about various political issues. Initially he's open to lots of ideas and eagerly gathers information. However, once he makes up his mind, he becomes stubborn and won't allow anything different to challenge his opinion. He's quite loud in voicing his viewpoints.

Now in his later years, Larry longs to transfer his knowledge to an apprentice. One after another came to the salon, stayed a few months and left because he is difficult to work for. They complained that he's indifferent to how people feel. He thinks others are too emotional. He is logical, rational, competitive, and a bit narcissistic, yet he lacks insight as to the impact his behavior has on his staff.

Candidly, Larry dislikes social events and family gatherings. He would rather be arguing politics with a colleague than exchanging personal information. Twice divorced, living alone suits him as he can surround himself with what he values most: books and technology. Researching the web makes him feel powerful, and he never makes a purchase without reading every bit of information he can find. He doesn't mind spending more if he thinks the item will last longer.

Find out your dominant Buying Style. Take the AlikeAbility ScoreCard at

CompellingSellingBook.com/resources

CHAPTER 3

WORDS THAT SELL TO EACH BUYING STYLE

Have you had a sales conversation and noticed the other person look away? Instantly, you knew that you lost rapport. Words can either attract or repel. When you can select the right expression based on the buyer's style, you will connect quickly and authentically with your prospects. Listen closely to their words, and they will teach you what to say (or write) that will lead to their doing business with you.

Words That Sell
to #2 Successful Buyers

For the #2 Buyer, make sure to deliver the words with energy, enthusiasm, and excitement. Add exclamation points to your correspondence. Bullets are especially effective as this buyer prefers texting over emails.

Words That Sell to #2 Successful Buyers (Transactional Sellers)

Style	Values	Synonyms
Successful Buyers	Freedom	Independence Free Will Spontaneous
	Action	Achieve Accomplish Command
	Excitement	Enthusiasm Eagerness Delight Elation
	Competition	Winning Successful Champion
	Image	Status Prestige Exclusive
	Adventure	Exploit Exploration Quest
	Experience	Opportunity High Risk, High Reward It's What's Happening
	Trendy	Hip Cool Fashionable

Words That Sell to #2 Successful Buyers (Transactional Sellers)		
Style	**Values**	**Synonyms**
Successful Buyers	Outstanding	Dazzling Exceptional Remarkable Unique
	Spontaneity	Impulsive Unplanned Free spirited
	Speed	Quick Fast Urgent
	Fun	Celebration Game Recreation
	Extraordinary	Different Exclusive Rare
	Exceptional	Noteworthy Phenomenal Singular
	Celebration	Bash Party Blowout Spree
	Energetic	Animated Vibrant Explosive

Examples of How to Use
Words That Sell to #2 Successful Buyers

Here are a few examples of how to use Words That Sell to #2 Successful Buyers:

- You'll **dazzle** prospects and create an **outstanding** impression when you **exploit** *Compelling Selling: Simple & Profitable Tips for Effective, Efficient Sales Conversations* to **win** their business and succeed.

- How **cool** is it to **command** the best words to use to acquire new customers!

- **Act now!** Don't miss out!

- Be the **best**!

- Be **first**!

- **New, improved.**

- **Amazing, awesome, indescribable!**

Words That Sell
to #4 Harmonious Buyers

While high energy and drama feed the #2 Buyer, they are a turn-off for the rest of the buyers.

#4 Buyers prefer a folksy, conversational approach. They are down-to-earth, casual people who don't stand on ceremony or carry pretenses. Hence the words and phrases must be selected with their values in mind.

A warm, friendly tone is very appealing. They like stories that feature people working together for the good of humankind. When you share personal information and do so from your heart, you create an instant bond and connection.

Run-on sentences, streams of consciousness, gushy monologues, and lots of emojis tell the #4 Buyer that you're like them. Ask questions about them and listen with interest. More than your words, this will communicate your sincerity.

Words That Sell to #4 Harmonious Buyers (Relational Sellers)		
Style	**Values**	**Synonyms**
Harmonious Buyers	Relationship	Connection Affiliation Rapport Togetherness Team
	Authenticity	Genuine True Real Trustworthy
	Significance	Meaning Importance Worth Magnitude World-Changing
	Harmony	Peace Agreement Accord Collaboration
	Ethics	Morality Right
	Casual	Informal Laid Back Down-to-Earth
	Comfortable	Ease Relaxed Contented
	Friendship	Alliance Companionship Camaraderie Closeness

Words That Sell to #4 Harmonious Buyers (Relational Sellers)		
Style	**Values**	**Synonyms**
	Bond	Link Union Attachment Tie
	Nurture	Grow Care for Provide
	Share	Contribute Partake Help
	Participate	Cooperate Collaborate Engage
	Support	Hold Carry Aid Help Volunteer
	Encourage	Reassure Motivate Comfort
	Minister	Foster Heal Treat
	Story	Narrative Dialogue Conversation

Examples of How to Use
Words That Sell to #4 Harmonious Buyers

Here are a few examples of how to use Words That Sell to #4 Harmonious Buyers:

- It's **important** for me to get to know you **personally**, help you **feel comfortable** and **relaxed** so that we can work together and **make a difference** using *Compelling Selling: Simple & Profitable Tips for Effective, Efficient Sales Conversations.*

- I **genuinely care** about how you **feel** as we reach a **harmonious** agreement about what's **right** for you.

- How do you **feel**?

- How can I be of **service**?

- **Let's** get to **know each other**.

- Me too! That also happened to me. **I feel the same way.**

- May I **share** my **story**?

Words That Sell
to #6 Orderly Buyers

#6 Buyers dislike over-the-top emotion. They also refrain from revealing personal information unless it's necessary. So the words and phrases used with the #2 and #4 Buyers do not connect with them.

Instead, it's important that you keep things on a formal level. Arriving early tells #6 Buyers that you respect and keep commitments. Have an agenda that you state and follow.

Communicate that you're professional by having your paperwork present and organized. Practice good manners and courtesy. Never interrupt!

Refer to your years of experience or the credentials you hold. #6 Buyers respect outside authorities and any titles and licenses you have earned. They appreciate testimonials from other clients as proof of low risk.

The words you use should reflect orderliness, structure, and rules. Write or talk in complete sentences and full paragraphs. Punctuate, conjugate, and spell correctly.

Words That Sell to #6 Orderly Buyers (Procedural Sellers)		
Style	**Values**	**Synonyms**
Orderly Buyers	Stability	Consistency Steadiness Strong
	Planning	Preparation Proposals Blueprints Budget Prediction Step-by-Step Process
	Rules	Instructions Directions Procedures Policies Regulations
	Tradition	Conventions Customs Rituals Practices Habits
	Credentials	Degrees Qualifications Certifications Testimonials Social Proof
	Classic	Timeless Time-honored Enduring
	Conventional	Fundamental Basic Moderate

Words That Sell to #6 Orderly Buyers (Procedural Sellers)		
Style	**Values**	**Synonyms**
Orderly Buyers	Safety	Protection Refuge Well-being
	Security	Guarantee Insurance Tried and True
	Manage	Administer Conduct Supervise Operate Oversee
	Orderliness	Arrangement Classification Design
	Routine	Everyday Normal Ordinary
	Periodic	Annual Recurrent Regular
	Predictable	Certain Foreseeable Anticipated
	Control	Discipline Government Restraint
	Reference	Policy Guarantee Principle

Examples of How to Use
Words That Sell to #6 Orderly Buyers

Here are a few examples of how to use Words That Sell to #6 Orderly Buyers:

- Over 300 **testimonials** demonstrate that *Compelling Selling: Simple & Profitable Tips for Effective, Efficient Sales Conversations* is organized to **guarantee** results when used **consistently**.

- It's a **tried and true system** that provides the **direction** needed to close more sales.

- Having over **25 years experience**, I hold **degrees** in psychology and social work and have been **certified** in sales training and adult learning.

- Pat had a similar experience and found our services to resolve the situation **effectively** and **efficiently**.

- Here's the **agenda** I prepared to get us **started**. Does this **cover** all the points you p**lanned** to raise?

- I offer a **money-back guarantee**.

Words That Sell
to #8 Educated Buyers

#8 Buyers want information. They prefer reading rather than listening. In either case, asking and answering questions compels these individuals to engage.

Facts, statistics, dimensions, research results, graphs, tables, and other types of tools that convey data fascinate and attract them. They are free thinkers and prefer to make up their own minds.

While #2 likes a bottom line statement, #8 Buyers must simultaneously understand the inner workings and form a big picture of the topic.

#6 Buyers seek an historical outlook, while #8 Buyers revel in scientific studies. They solve problems and look for practical and utilitarian approaches.

They appreciate clever word choices and a good vocabulary.

Words That Sell to #8 Educated Buyers (Informational Sellers)		
Style	**Values**	**Synonyms**
Educated Buyers	Learning	Knowledge Author Education Teacher
	Intelligence	Savvy Smart Educated Brainpower
	Competence	Know-How Expertise Skilled
	Big Picture Thinking	Universal Truths General Principles Theory Logic
	Science	Research Study Technology Reason
	Information	Facts Statistics Technology Research
	Solution	Answer Explanation Result
	Practical	Realistic Pragmatic Feasible

Words That Sell to #8 Educated Buyers (Informational Sellers)		
Style	**Values**	**Synonyms**
Educated Buyers	Utilitarian	Useful Functional Suitable
	Data	Evidence Statistics Compilations
	Facts	Clues Numbers Score Reality
	Feedback	Assessment Evaluation Observation
	Advancement	Growth Improvement Upgrading
	Think	Consider Determine Calculate Analyze
	Analysis	Scrutiny Investigation Dissection
	Precision	Accuracy Exact Meticulous

Examples of How to Use
Words That Sell to #8 Educated Buyers

Here are a few examples of how to use Words That Sell to #8 Educated Buyers:

- I **know** you'll want to **read** *Compelling Selling: Simple & Profitable Tips for Effective, Efficient Sales Conversations* thoroughly because it provides the **scientific approach** needed to become a master of sales conversations. It's **practical**, **functional**, and **comprehensive information** in a convenient reference book.

- **Read** about this **solution** to the **problem** about what's **realistic** to say to all buying styles.

- What **questions** do you have?

- What **information** do you need?

- You'll find **answers** on this website along with several **articles** on the topic.

- Here's a **white paper** that has the **raw data** as well as an **explanation** of how this approach works.

- I created this **model** to show the **correlation** between these **ideas**.

Into Action

As you read through these tables and examples, you noted how different the words and phrases are for each style. That's because they stem from different values.

When you use the right words with the right Buyer's Style, you get results—powerful, masterful, awesome, heart-felt results.

Maureen, a website developer and #4 Relational Seller, had an appointment with a prospect who had been referred by a business colleague. She went online and looked at his profile.

Her immediate impression was that Roger was a jet-setter. His photographs showed a man who liked adventures, and his copy was sparse. His clothing and haircut indicated that he liked to dress fashionably. Roger was a #2 Buyer.

With this analysis in mind, Maureen knew to expect him to be time-sensitive, driven for quick results, and resistant to collaboration. Understanding some of his values, she approached the meeting prepared to move quickly, outline briefly her services, and ask for the sale on the first meeting.

She talked about creating a winning design, giving his company a decided advantage, and providing extraordinary presence. On the spot he hired her.

In another example, Angelique, a financial planner and #6 Seller (Procedural), needed the right words to secure an appointment with a prospect who managed a 25-person law firm that could potentially refer a lot of business to her.

She researched his buying style and noted that he had just one photo of himself that he used both on his website and LinkedIn profile. His first email response had no salutation, was blunt, and logical. Given his occupation, lack of social media posts, and correspondence, she concluded that he was probably a #8 Buyer.

Typically. Angelique would have followed up by sending a detailed presentation of her services with a proper cover letter. Instead, she put aside pleasantries and asked him a direct question: *Does it make sense for us to meet?* He answered in the affirmative and she was invited to meet with his staff.

Finally, Justin, a consultant and #8 Seller (Informational), usually introduces himself to prospects with a lengthy email about his company and solutions. However, Jennifer, a serial entrepreneur, was a #2 Buyer. Taking my suggestion, his email was just 3 lines:

1. I am a marketing expert and strategist.
2. I have a business opportunity for you.
3. Are you interested?

She replied that day, and they made an appointment. And he got a new client.

To get hired, you must read your prospect's buying style and speak that language.

CHAPTER 4

DIAGNOSING BUYING STYLES

Knowing the words people use is a good starting point for diagnosing your prospect's buying style. The sooner you figure out someone's way of communicating and making decisions, the sooner you can shift to match that style with authenticity.

Here are the 6 major ways I teach my clients to identify the 4 Buying Styles in less than a minute. How individuals:

1. Talk
2. Dress
3. Behave
4. Correspond
5. Post on social media
6. Decorate their home and office

Vocal Qualities

I'm starting with how people talk because, during times of social distancing, often the first contact you have with a prospect is a phone call. Perhaps you are receiving inbound calls (especially if your website is optimized for search engines), having virtual coffee meets, or telephoning a list of leads.

While there are many types of vocal qualities, you need to pay attention to only three of them: speed, volume, and inflection.

#2 Successful Buyers talk loud and fast with very little inflection. If you remember, they're usually in a hurry to get things done to have more adventures and experiences. As a listener, you hear a directive tone.

If they think they know the gist of what's being said, these people interrupt and shift the conversation to the next idea. They take command and act in charge. You might sense a demand.

#4 Harmonious Buyers also tend to have good volume and speak quickly. However, they use lots of inflection. Inflection occurs when the voice goes up and down the scale and draws out words and syllables. It sounds almost musical, and the tone you hear is warm and friendly.

They use lots of nonverbal sounds (hmmm) to encourage the speaker, and they interrupt. In this case, the interruption is intended to share how they identify with the speaker, not to divert the conversation to another topic.

Have you tried to say "goodbye" to #4 Harmonious Buyers? They dislike endings and have just one more thing to say. These individuals like to stay in connection.

#6 Orderly Buyers are moderate across the board. In comparison to the last two styles, they speak slower and softer. Like #4 Harmonious Buyers, they also use inflection. Their tone is pleasant and formal.

#6 Orderly Buyers are prone to speak in full sentences and complete paragraphs. They take turns when speaking and strongly dislike being interrupted. One oddity I've noticed is that they will say "I'm sorry" when interrupted, probably because the rules have been broken.

#8 Educated Buyers are slower in speech and have quiet voices. They rarely use inflection. The lack of inflection is heard as a monotone. Hence, their tone is one of authority, and they sound like a science professor.

A big characteristic is the pause. They are slow to respond as they seek to find the precise words and phrasing. These are the people who always ask questions, deep profound questions so they can understand how the world works.

Appearance

Seeing prospects in person greatly enhances your ability to diagnose their style because you can look at their clothing, including shoes and accessories. Notice their appearance, the choice of colors, patterns, and overall look.

#2 Successful Buyers are fashion-forward and enjoy showing off their stylish, new wardrobe. Although they are comfortable wearing bright colors, big patterns, and bold accessories, even when they appear in neutrals, such as all black, they display a statement piece that makes them stand out.

For men, it could be a hat, tie and hanky, boots, belt buckle, cufflinks, monogrammed shirt, and eyeglass frames. Women wear tight or revealing clothing, stilettos, dangle earrings, gems and jewels, precious metals, and outstanding makeup. Both men and women have manicures, styled hair and even hair pieces. Body piercings and body art are also a common form of self-expression.

#2 Successful Buyers enjoy dressing up. At the same time, they can also make a strong statement by being underdressed. They bring the "cool" factor by wearing cutoffs, torn and ripped jeans and shirts. Their unbuttoned blouses and shirts can be seen as sexy and provocative.

#4 Harmonious Buyers choose comfort over fashion. The shirt or blouse hangs over the waistline and is open at the neck. They prefer loose clothing made from soft fabrics. Sweaters and sweater vests, ponchos and similar items are a staple in their wardrobe.

Their shoes are well-worn and without laces. Women prefer low heels. Barefoot is always an option!

Small patterns and color is acceptable with a nod towards pastels and earth tones.

#6 Orderly Buyers take excellent care of their clothing. Regardless of the time of day, they look like they just walked out of the dry cleaners. Shoes are polished, trousers creased, and belt, socks and shoes coordinated. Never would their clothing have any stains or defects.

Because they follow the rules for proper attire, they dress up rather than dress down for most occasions. They stick with timeless, classic colors and style: neutral colors for pants, skirts, and jackets with a white or pastel shirt or blouse.

They prefer plain colors and limit patterns and accessories to those that are small and discreet.

#8 Educated Buyers care little about fashion. Choosing what to wear is a practical matter. The easiest way to solve this problem is copy the #6

Orderly Buyers because they know the "rules." However, #8 Educated Buyers make a big exception. They can't be bothered pressing their clothes, polishing footwear, and matching accessories and shoes to their outfit.

In selecting items, they pay for quality because it lasts longer. They intend to and do wear their clothing, shoes, and accessories until they are worn out. That means that some things may be out-of-date. The result is that their overall appearance looks "off."

Other than a wedding band, neither gender tends to wear much jewelry and makeup. Their eyeglass frames are plain. A lack of hairstyle is another telltale sign of #8 Educated Buyers. If they wear patterns, it's usually geometric prints.

Behavior

Of all the kinds of behaviors to notice, I'm going to focus on just a couple: arrival time and greetings. If you go back to their primary values, I'm sure you can identify many other traits. My clients and I have fun applying the principles of each style to specific situations and activities.

#2 Successful Buyers arrive late. There are many reasons for this behavior. Often, they overbook their schedules so that they can do more but fail to take into account the amount of time needed between activities. While they do their best to arrive on time, a tight schedule means roaring into the parking lot at the stroke of the hour when the appointment begins. Hence, they arrive late.

I think a subtle reason is being late also allows them to make a grand appearance. People notice them. And since nothing "important" can take place without them, they believe no harm has happened. Consequently, they rarely apologize for any delays. Immediately they jump in and participate.

#2 Successful Buyers are full of energy. Rather than a handshake, they like to greet others with a high five, knuckle flare, or chest bump. How someone reciprocates quickly shows whether they are the same style.

Just like #2 Successful Buyers, #4 Harmonious Buyers arrive late. But . . . they always have an excuse. Because they find it hard to let go of one relationship, even though shortly they expect to be meeting with another person, they get a "late" start. Other reasons for their lateness include helping someone, letting pedestrians and other drivers pass, or taking care of friends, family and colleagues. Behind each excuse is their caretaking of others.

#4 Harmonious Buyers love to touch and enjoy hugging. In a business setting, this show of affection may be inappropriate. Instead, they place a hand on top of your hand, arm, or shoulder to add connection to a handshake. Moreover, they pump your hand repeatedly to maintain contact and increase connectivity. That person who warns you, "I'm a hugger" and then embraces you without permission is decidedly a #4 Harmonious Buyer.

#6 Orderly Buyers arrive 10–20 minutes early. They believe that for the meeting to begin on time, they must come early to find a parking place, walk to the designated office, use the restroom, get water or coffee, check email or do other things in preparation so that the appointment starts on time.

They take offense when things are delayed and do a slow, inward burn. Being late is unacceptable and can result in the seller losing the deal. This tendency can be a huge factor in causing strained relations between the styles.

#6 Orderly Buyers greet people formally. First they look you directly in your eyes, offer their hand, shake yours once with moderate pressure, drop the hand, and drop their eyes. Those are the rules of being proper.

#8 Educated Buyers usually arrive just in time. They don't like to be early as it might require chitchat, which they despise. As in other conventions, they mimic the behavior of #6 Orderly Buyers UNLESS it's illogical. They are quick to break the rules when it makes sense and suits them.

Because they dislike touch, they would prefer to greet someone by nodding, bowing, or in some other nonphysical way. #8 Educated Buyers also shy away from direct eye contact. They rarely offer their hand but do take yours, without much energy. If you have ever had a limp handshake, it's probably with #8 Educated Buyers.

Correspondence

Since the majority of this book is focused on the right words to use with each buying style, it stands to reason that you can easily identify the exact style by the words they use in their correspondence. I'll add just a few additional characteristics to make the differences more apparent.

#2 Successful Buyers are not much for reading or writing. Instead, their correspondence consists of bullet points and texting. Acronyms are a lifesaver as they reduce time and effort. With voice recognition software becoming better at conveying messages, they would rather dictate than type. Spelling errors, incomplete phrases, garbled messages are commonplace for them.

#4 Harmonious Buyers are eager to form relationships and bond with others. While they prefer to talk, writing is an acceptable alternative. They can get carried away and write a lot. Adding emojis allows them to express their feelings and connect with the reader. Inspiration quotes, motivational messages, words of wisdom dot their correspondence.

When #6 Orderly Buyers communicate, they follow all the rules of grammar, syntax, and spelling. They write in full sentences and complete paragraphs. They spell out acronyms and may even avoid using contractions.

#8 Educated Buyers are writers and have often published their work or at least blogs or articles online. Invariably they reference this accomplishment. One of their strange quirks is the lack of a greeting or salutation. They plunge directly into the content of their message and just exit when finished.

Social Media Presence

Posting on social media often consists of both photos and pictures along with captions and words. Knowing how someone dresses can help you figure out their buying style along with the words they use and manner of correspondence. Review the clues mentioned above.

As you might have guessed, the frequency and amount of posts varies with buying style. Certain social media platforms appeal to specific buying styles. One other factor can also be used to form a guess as to your prospect's buying style. It's their occupation.

- Which ones allow for someone to make quick decisions, take charge, and be on stage? These attract #2 Successful Buyers.

- Which professions provide a source of connection and affiliation? #4 Harmonious Buyers are drawn to these.

- What types of work require following and enforcing rules? These jobs appeal to #6 Orderly Buyers.

- What occupations depend on thorough research and analysis? #8 Educated Buyers prefer these tasks.

While the answers to the above questions provide a big clue as to the person's buying style, keep in mind that everyone is a blend of all 4 styles.

#2 Successful Buyers love the recognition that social media provides. Simultaneously, they dislike spending lots of time writing and posting. Twitter is a perfect solution because of the limited characters permitted per post.

They like to "show off" for the camera, and you'll notice their striking poses or zany facial expressions. Selfies are perfect for them! Always into action, you'll find them being photographed with celebrities or high-status individuals. And you'll see posts featuring travel and adventures.

Being connected to lots of people and being able to write without restriction makes Facebook perfect for #4 Harmonious Buyers. They like to provide daily status reports and post informal photos of themselves, kids, and animals. So Instagram and Pinterest also provide this vehicle.

Besides lots of friends and family, they love to repost other people's messages. They are quick to like, compliment, and encourage others. When you spot emojis and gifs in abundance, you have found #4 Harmonious Buyers.

In contrast, #6 Orderly Buyers regulate their appearance on social media. They participate moderately and with reserve. Photos are mostly posed, and they keep their personal life fairly private. There is no one platform that most appeals as they dislike publicizing their activities.

What's notable is how they present on LinkedIn. They answer almost every category on their profiles and write out their thoughts completely. They list their degrees, certifications, licenses, and honors. Next to their name, they make sure to list their earned credentials.

#8 Educated Buyers tend to sidestep social media unless they can demonstrate their knowledge and expertise. They shun showing off or being in the limelight. Rarely will you see photographs of them. If caught by the camera, they offer no smile and seem uncomfortable with the experience.

LinkedIn offers them a good platform for sharing information. Twitter allows them to display their smarts in expressing an idea within a limited number of characters. Another outlet to demonstrate their competence is YouTube IF they have a high degree of #2 Successful Buyers as well. Otherwise, they rarely post.

Decor

Not every seller has the privilege or opportunity of viewing their prospects in their home and/or office. Those that do can confirm their guess about the person's buying style by noting the way individuals decorate their personal spaces.

#2 Successful Buyers surround themselves with the "BEST." They choose things that are sleek, modern, and expensive. Whenever possible, their possessions bear designer labels. The decor speaks "expensive."

When working, they have lots of tabs open on their computers, plenty of papers strewn around their desk, various items and knickknacks out and about. However, they want outsiders to perceive them as being "cool." To achieve the minimalist look, they stuff a drawer, closet, or other type of container with their belongings.

Modern art might be displayed. #2 Successful Buyers will also hang photos of themselves receiving an award or being seen with a celebrity.

#4 Harmonious Buyers put comfort first and are relaxed about their environments. Their space is clean but not neat. Piles of items fill tables, desks, and surfaces. They know that the sought-after item is there, just not sure where. They struggle with organization.

They select oversized furnishings with soft textiles. Matching is not the goal. They place family photos prominently on desks and walls, gallery style. Often there is an abundance of knickknacks, all of which have a story and sentimental value.

Having things clean, organized, and in good condition characterize the work and home spaces of #6 Orderly Buyers. Everything has its place and is put away. The items might also be labeled for easy finding. A single, tasteful photo of the family might be displayed.

Diplomas, licenses, and certifications have been framed and hung on the wall. They choose classic furniture and matching window treatments. They may have heirloom items as well.

#8 Educated Buyers are indifferent to their personal space as they are to their personal appearance. They select furnishings that wear well and have a long life. The biggest characteristic is their extensive collection of books. They surround themselves with reading matter.

Because they value information so highly, like the #4 Harmonious Buyers, #8 Educated Buyers may have piles of papers. However, they know exactly where the document resides. Their spaces have the latest technology, and they know how to program and use it.

If you want to discuss how to apply this to an important prospect and receive valuable tips on building rapport and getting hired, book a complimentary Discovery Call. Use this convenient link:

NancyZare.YouCanBook.me

CHAPTER 5

FOLLOWING UP WITH EACH BUYING STYLE

As you dive into understanding and working with the 4 Buying Styles, you'll quickly realize that subtle shifts are required in order to apply the Platinum Rule: Treat others the way they want to be treated. Not only should you alter the words and phrases you use but also the approach. Let me illustrate with an essential sales activity: follow up.

Did you know that less than 2% of sales occur during the first contact?

The vast majority of buyers need at least 2 touch points to go forward; and 80% need 7 or more contacts! Jim Rohn, great American motivational speaker, said, "The fortune is in the follow-up." Obviously. Yet 48% never follow up even once, and 88% of professionals stop after 3 tries!

If you're the sort of person who is concerned about being perceived as pushy and aggressive, you may be minimizing your follow-up activities. Most people who score high as #4 Harmonious Buyers are especially sensitive to being viewed as salesy, and many individuals who rank first as #8 Educated Buyers dislike selling outright.

I know how important it is to these individuals to maintain integrity and self-esteem. It is totally in alignment to serve your prospects by developing relationships based on the way they prefer to be treated. Potential clients expect you to adjust to their way of doing things. If you don't, they are unlikely to hire you.

I have found a simple means for following up that is noninvasive and is always well received. It keeps you top of mind without being in someone's space. Plus, it's easy to do. Send a greeting card with a single sentence.

"I appreciate you."

#4 Harmonious Buyers find this method easy to adopt because they "naturally" compliment the other party as a fundamental part of their style. #8 Educated Buyers see the correlation between appreciation and sales. The law of reciprocity is convincing testimony about the value of this approach.

As for #6 Orderly Buyers, think of this as a system. Step 1: the initial meeting. Step 2: follow up with a message of appreciation. Step 3: continue to express gratitude as a matter of course.

Finally, #2 Successful Buyers can view expressing appreciation as a "game" in which the odds favor you when you pause to appreciate prospects and customers. Appreciation can help you stand out from the crowd and thus "win" the sale. Be warned, however, that appreciation without authenticity can backfire.

It's worth repeating. The formula to follow up without being seen as pushy and aggressive is to tell your potential buyer each step of the way, "I appreciate you."

Now let's examine how to follow up more specifically with designs and messages for each type of buyer.

#2 Successful Buyers

#2 Successful Buyers are quick decision-makers. Usually they make up their minds on the spot. Even though only 2% of sales occur on the first contact, don't hesitate to ask for the sale during the initial meeting!

Of course, just as quickly as they say "yes," #2 Successful Buyers can jump into another opportunity. That means you must stay top of mind. Periodic text messages work as well as your being highly visible on social media. By creating the impression that you're doing exciting things and seen everywhere, this heightens your reputation in their eyes. These people like to hang out with the "cool" cats and rub shoulders with celebrities.

#2 Successful Buyers often crave attention and bask in recognition. Be sure to applaud their exploits and accomplishments. Since they usually post regularly on social media, become a fan. Express excitement and engage with them.

Here's the link to learn more about my suggestions on how to follow up with the #2 Successful Buyers:

CompellingSellingBook.com/resources

#4 Harmonious Buyers

#4 Harmonious Buyers are a relatively quick decision -maker. Show that you care, and they will most likely follow you with blind faith. Be interested in their personal and family life. Be open to sharing about yours. To win their trust, you must be willing to share about yours. This genuine exchange is bound to result in making a friend.

Remember that they are buying a relationship with you, not the service or products you provide.

Human-interest stories gain their attention. They also want to be a part of the team, contribute to the community and support worthy causes. Let them know about any charitable work you do because #4

Harmonious Buyers are motivated to support you and your efforts.

Follow-up is crucial with the #4 Harmonious Buyers because they often get buyer's remorse. They are extremely sensitive about being treated as a transaction. If they sense this is true, they cancel appointments, no show, and return the purchase. Within 24 hours of saying "yes," you must reconnect and assure them that it's the relationship that matters, not the sale.

Here's the link to learn more about my suggestions on how to follow up with the #4 Harmonious Buyers:

CompellingSellingBook.com/resources

#6 Orderly Buyers

#6 Orderly Buyers are relatively slow decision-makers. They require social proof—testimonies from other satisfied users—before they commit to you. This is the person who checks out your status with the Better Business Bureau and other professional associations or neighborhood forums.

Being professional and organized goes a long way in solidifying a relationship with them. Give them advanced notice when you plan to phone or visit. And be sure to arrive early to any appointment. Be formal and sequential in your follow-up activities with #6 Orderly Buyers.

Although they take a number of contacts before going forward, they hate change. So they tend to be "true blue" and loyal. Since they rely on testimonies from satisfied customers, #6 Orderly Buyers can be a good source of referrals once they have enough experience with your product or service.

Here's the link to learn more about my suggestions on how to follow up with the #6 Orderly Buyers:

CompellingSellingBook.com/resources

#8 Educated Buyers

#8 Educated Buyers are the slowest to make a buying decision. Hence, you need a follow-up system that you implement consistently over time. The best approach is a drip campaign in which you send a small bit of information every few days or weeks.

Although they take a while to decide, once they come to a conclusion, they stick with it. In fact, the #8 Educated Buyers can be downright stubborn. They don't mind spending more IF you can show them that their investment solves a problem in the long run.

These individuals also tend to exert considerable influence within their circle. That's because they have acquired a reputation as being "smart" and having done their homework. Other styles, especially #4 Buyers, are prone to follow their lead. So cultivating a relationship with the #8 Educated Buyers is worth the investment of time and your efforts to follow up.

I've prepared a video link on following up with the #8 Educated Buyers:

CompellingSellingBook.com/resources

Follow Up with Cards

Following up takes two forms: digital and tangible. Given the high speed and low cost of digital marketing, many people opt for ways to follow up that are digital. These include leaving a voice message, sending a text or personal message, and crafting emails, either individually or as a series.

The ways to follow up that are tangible require more time and personal connection. Hence, they are more expensive. Meeting in person, providing a gift, and sending a physical card fall into this category.

Remember how your mother insisted you write a thank you note for each present you received? Grudgingly, you may have jotted a few words, signed your name, and addressed the envelope. Despite how you may have felt in taking this action, each card won points for manners and etiquette. In comparison to years past, her advice is even more relevant today in this digital era when people long for human connection. Listen to your Mama! Start sending gratitude cards.

Sending a tangible card is the most neglected yet powerful way of following up with prospects (and customers). Only 11% of emails are opened in comparison to 100% of cards. While phone messages increasingly go to voicemail, and text messages can be intrusive and demanding, a heartfelt card can be savored and saved for days, weeks, months, and even years to come.

I urge you to send a card as part of your follow-up system. It will make you stand out from the competition, stay top of mind without coming across as salesy, bring excitement, delight, and surprise to the recipient, and touch people emotionally.

To make card sending match your prospect's style, here are some suggestions about design, color, and message.

#2 Successful Buyers are captured by bling and humor. Select cards that are dramatic and over the top. Bright colors, snappy words, and embellishments work. They LOVE to see their mug shots on the front cover of the card. A frame around it such as "Time Magazine's Person of the Year" is totally in keeping with their style.

#4 Harmonious Buyers seek connection and emotion. Cards that display babies, pets, flowers, and nature grab their hearts. Express yourself freely. Use the "L" words as appropriate (Like, Love, Laugh,

Live). A card that displays family photos will be treasured.

#6 Orderly Buyers prefer formality and reserve. A simple message or a patriotic photo on a card communicates effectively with them. Unless you know them well, avoid putting a photo of them or their family in the card. A company logo is a better choice.

#8 Educated Buyers prefer content over sentiment. Choose a card with a quotation or saying. Plain -Jane works well as they don't like to stand out. If they happen to be an author, I strongly suggest putting their book jacket on the card.

If you want to discuss how to follow up with an important prospect, book a complimentary Discovery Call. Use this convenient link:

NancyZare.YouCanBook.me

CHAPTER 6

PUTTING THESE IDEAS INTO PRACTICE

The AlikeAbility System not only identifies buying styles but also selling styles. Most people sell the way they buy. Occasionally, they use a different style, just like they change styles going from a work to a social situation.

In the same way that there are 4 buying styles, there are also 4 selling styles. These correspond to how people communicate. There are:

- Transactional Sellers
- Relational Sellers
- Procedural Sellers
- Informational Sellers

Transactional Sellers

Transactional Sellers, like #2 Buyers, share a love for speed and action. Selling is a game, one that they intend to win. The goal is to enroll prospects as quickly as possible and go on to the next challenge, especially if they are paid on commission or are incentivized by rewards.

Because of their desire to triumph, they are drawn to selling as an occupation. They bask in recognition and applause. Transactional Sellers often succeed because they play the numbers game, which is this: If you talk to enough people, and ask for the sale, a certain percentage will say "Yes."

While Transactional Sellers have many strengths, when allowed full reign, they can turn off the other 3 styles. Because they are focused primarily on making the sale quickly, they may neglect the importance of building relationships. They are impatient when prospects have questions, ask for details, and want time to exchange personal information.

In their desire to secure this client so they can move on to the next one, Transactional Sellers look for ways to automate or take shortcuts. Hence, they use bots and other preprogrammed outreach and follow-up activities. For them, it's all about numbers and reaching more people.

Transactional Sellers place a low regard on specific information and tend to gloss over things. Their enthusiasm can be interpreted as hype. In these and other ways, they put off the slower decision-making styles. As a result, others view them as being pushy and aggressive.

Relational Sellers

Relational Sellers tend to focus on the relationship. Their natural love for and curiosity about people quickly puts others at ease. They readily provide emotional support, especially when discussing difficult issues.

Relational Sellers are curious to know about the prospect and enjoy exchanging personal information. They exude trustworthiness as they listen intently to prospective customers. They are in no rush to consummate the deal. AND that is precisely one of their biggest mistakes as a seller.

Their friendliness may overlap with the service they offer to the point that Relational Sellers may find themselves coaching the prospect and offering support rather than asking for the sale. Why? It's because they dislike rejection, tension, and conflict.

Relational Sellers accept and identify too easily with the buyer's stories and also their excuses for not going forward. They have a tendency to take rejection personally. This is especially apparent when it comes to stating their fees as they may offer a discount, reduce their commissions, and even give away services with the hope of making the sale.

The other communication styles view them as being a pushover, a door mat, indecisive, and lacking in leadership. They are uncomfortable when a business conversation seems personal. Relational Sellers are doing themselves a disservice by their concessions.

Procedural Sellers

Procedural Sellers stick to the script. With a firm agenda in mind, they have a go-to method for opening sales conversations. It begins with a brief exchange of pleasantries and then down to business. They take things seriously and act responsibly.

Providing the buyer with the background of the service, product, and company is paramount in the eyes of Procedural Sellers. They expect that people need time to investigate their reputation and claims. They work at a steady pace and make sure they have covered all the details.

Procedural Sellers feel duty-bound to follow the rules and adhere to the system. They are insecure when invited to deviate from the way they learned to do things and have difficulty adjusting to change. Their cautiousness and desire to avoid mistakes keep them from seizing opportunities and taking on new challenges.

To the other communication styles, Procedural Sellers are perceived as being rigid and inflexible. They seem to lack speed, empathy, and logic.

Informational Sellers

Speaking of logic, that's one of the main attributes of Informational Sellers. They are focused primarily on education and making sure that they convey what they know about their field.

Informational Sellers are excellent listeners. Their keen minds gather lots of data, ask profound questions, and analyze all the facts. They do extensive research about their subject area with the desire of becoming an expert. Yet they shy away from accepting that title and humbly admit to knowing only a little.

They think deeply about what they learn. Informational Sellers are constantly taking courses, acquiring new skills, getting additional certifications and licenses in their field. They have the answer or will find it. More than any other selling style, they do their due diligence.

Although it is their strength, striving to know everything is also their weakness. When it comes to sales, Informational Sellers are so thorough in explaining everything that prospects feel overwhelmed and overloaded. Because information is so important to their decision-making process, they provide it in abundance.

Feeling urgency or deadlines upset their sensibilities, and they assume prospects respond similarly. In fact, Informational Sellers tend to avoid asking for the sale because they don't want the prospect to be pressured.

Informational Sellers often say, "I hate to sell" and resign themselves to thinking sales is not for them. Consequently, they tend to be hands-off and passive with prospects to the extent that they fail to read buying signals.

While these are some of the common pitfalls for the various selling styles, the most common mistake made by 95% of sellers is the *inability to adjust their communication style to that of the prospect*. They are stuck in only one way of communicating, one way of selling. To make more sales and acquire more customers and clients, you need to learn how to recognize your prospect's buying style and adjust yourself to it. You need AlikeAbility!

Because the majority of people fail to shift their selling style to match the buying style of their prospects, they play a numbers game, as I mentioned previously. You've probably heard the expression that sales IS a numbers game. That's because so many people remain stuck in their style of selling and communicating to the point that they are clueless that they need to make an adjustment.

If there are 4 buying styles and 4 selling styles, mathematically on average, you naturally match your prospect only one out of four times, or 25%. That means that a whopping 75% of the time, you're not speaking the language of your buyer!

Rather than adjust your communication, the solution for many people is to find and talk to more leads, hoping that the "right" one will appear. This is very costly and time intensive, not to mention the emotional wear and tear on you.

With each prospect you meet, your hopes rise and are then dashed when that person doesn't buy from you. It raises the old adage that insanity is doing the same thing and expecting different results. When you communicate and sell the way you always have, you continue to get the same results.

You may have realized that you have to do something different. Bottom line, if you desire to be more successful in sales, you must match your communication style to that of your client. By doing so, the prospect relaxes, feels comfortable, develops trust, lets go of sales resistance, and is open to doing business with you.

If you want to discuss how to apply this to an important prospect, book a complimentary Discovery Call with me. Use this convenient link:

NancyZare.YouCanBook.me

CHAPTER 7

COMMENCEMENT

I hope that you've found this information valuable, stimulating, and beneficial in developing sales relationships. Now that you have an understanding of the 4 Buying Styles, their values, the words to use, and how to follow up, you may be curious to apply these principles so you can get hired.

Yes, you can have a distinct edge in conversations and correspondence when you know the buyer's style and adjust your approach and words. Information without application is useless. You must put these ideas into practice, which I can help you do.

To explore your options, schedule a 30-minute Personal Sales Success Session. Use this convenient calendar link:

NancyZare.YouCanBook.me

I look forward to hearing your story of getting hired by identifying your prospect's style and matching it.

To your sales success,

Nancy

Dr. Nancy Zare

ABOUT DR. NANCY ZARE

I was born a psychologist, the last child and only girl into a family where my parents had serious marital issues. My earliest memory is hearing the cupboards bang, glasses break, doors slam, and loud voices quarreling.

Having witnessed at an early age how communication can tear people apart, I'm on the path to provide the "secret decoder ring" to understand other people and facilitate positive personal relations.

Originally from Cleveland, Ohio, I attended Boston University where I majored in psychology. Later I completed a master's degree and doctorate degree in social work at Boston College. I am also certified in sales training and adult education.

My career includes in-patient mental health, sales, college teaching, and public speaking. Using my knowledge of human behavior and experience in sales, I started Rapport Builderz, where I advise service-based entrepreneurs how to prospect online, open sales conversations, generate leads, follow up, and get hired.

I currently reside outside Boston, no spouse or pets at this moment, but I'm definitely looking to change that status! I hope to support your business growth by finding the exact words to use that connect quickly and authentically with your prospects and clients.

A SMALL FAVOR

Thank you for reading *Compelling Selling*! I am positive if you follow what I've written, you will be on your way to having better sales conversations.

I have a small, quick favor to ask. Would you mind taking a minute or two and leaving an honest review for this book on Amazon? Reviews are the BEST way to help others purchase this book, and I check all my reviews looking for helpful feedback. Visit:

CompellingSellingBook.com/review

If you have any questions or if you would just like to tell me what you think about *Compelling Selling*, shoot an email to Nancy@RapportBuilderz.com.

I'd love to hear from you!

DON'T FORGET YOUR GIFT!

Thank you for reading *Compelling Selling: Simple & Profitable Techniques for Effective, Efficient Sales Conversations.*

I appreciate you, and because you've taken the time to learn about the way people buy and the words you can use to connect with them quickly and authentically, I have a special gift for you. It's the AlikeAbility™ ScoreCard.

The ScoreCard gives you information about your Buying Style, your preferred way of messaging and receiving communication. Since we tend to sell the way we buy, it also provides a sneak preview into how you might normally approach prospects.

Knowing your dominant style will enable you to enjoy reading this book with a keen eye for:

- Learning how you behave.

- Learning how others perceive you.

- Figuring out where you differ from other styles.

- Determining your combination of the 4 Buying Styles.

- Other surprises about yourself, how you buy and sell.

It takes less than 5 minutes to complete! And the information lasts a lifetime! Visit:

CompellingSellingBook.com/resources